The Future of SEO: Strategies for Tomorrow

I0011163

About

With over 25 years of experience in the dynamic realm of digital marketing, this author has witnessed the internet's remarkable evolution from a novelty to a fundamental aspect of daily life. A dedicated SEO consultant, they specialize in navigating the complexities of shifting algorithms and enhancing online visibility, all while fostering sustainable growth for businesses. Their passion for continuous learning fuels a commitment to empowering others with actionable insights, whether for companies aiming to boost their search rankings or individuals seeking to demystify SEO. By blending data-driven strategies with a personalized touch, they emphasize that true success is about delivering value, engaging the right audience, and building lasting credibility in the digital landscape.

Table of Contents

1. Understanding SEO: The Foundation

2. The Role of Content in SEO

3. Technical SEO: The Backbone of Your Website

4. On-Page SEO Strategies

5. Off-Page SEO: Building Authority

10. Crafting an Effective SEO Strategy

(1) - 10.1 Setting Clear SEO Goals for Your Business

(2) - 10.2 Developing a Roadmap for Success

(3) - 10.3 Regularly Updating Your SEO Strategy

11. Mobile-First Indexing and Its Impact

(1) - 11.1 Understanding Mobile-First Indexing

(2) - 11.2 Best Practices for Mobile Optimization

(3) - 11.3 Tools to Test Mobile Friendliness

12. The Importance of User Experience (UX) in SEO

(1) - 12.1 How UX Impacts SEO Rankings

(2) - 12.2 Designing for the User Journey

(3) - 12.3 Measuring User Engagement Metrics

13. Navigating Algorithm Updates

(1) - 13.1 Understanding Google's Algorithm Changes

(2) - 13.2 How to Adapt to Major Updates

(3) - 13.3 Keeping Up with Future Trends

14. SEO Myths and Misconceptions

(1) - 14.1 Debunking Common SEO Myths

(2) - 14.2 The Truth About Keyword Stuffing

(3) - 14.3 Understanding the Role of Domain Age

15. Building a Sustainable SEO Plan

(1) - 15.1 The Importance of Consistency in SEO

(2) - 15.2 Balancing Short-Term and Long-Term Strategies

(3) - 15.3 Keeping abreast of Industry Trends and Changes

16. Importance of SEO Consulting

(1) - 16.1 The Importance of Good SEO Consulting

(2) - 16.2 About Author

1. Understanding SEO: The Foundation

1.1 What is SEO and Why is it Important?

Essentially, it involves making strategic decisions about how your site is structured, the content you produce, and the keywords you target. When you optimize your site for search engines like Google, you are trying to ensure that your pages are more relevant and valuable to users searching for information related to your business. The higher your website ranks on search engine results pages, the more likely visitors will find and click on your site. This means that investing time and resources into SEO can ultimately lead to increased visibility, more traffic, and greater engagement with your content.

For small businesses, it can be particularly impactful because they often operate in competitive niches and may not have the marketing budgets of larger corporations. SEO provides a level playing field; with the right strategies, even a small business can outshine larger competitors in search results. Making informed SEO decisions can help establish your online presence, build credibility, and foster lasting relationships with customers. By investing in SEO, you essentially plant the seeds for growth, as the benefits compound over time, leading to sustained organic traffic and increased sales without the need for continual ad spend.

Successful SEO requires understanding your audience, as it's not just about ranking high in search engines, but also connecting with the right users. If you can pinpoint what potential customers are searching for, you can tailor your website to meet those needs, resulting in a better user experience. Prioritizing SEO is not merely a technical task; it's about thinking critically about how to serve your audience effectively while simultaneously gaining visibility. An essential practical tip is to start conducting keyword research to identify what your ideal customers are searching for online. Tools like Google Keyword Planner or Ubersuggest can provide insights into keywords that drive traffic relevant to your business, setting the foundation for effective SEO efforts.

1.2 The Evolution of SEO: A Historical Perspective

In the early days of the internet, SEO was largely about cramming as many keywords as possible into a webpage. Many website owners believed that if they repeated certain words enough times, they would somehow rank higher in search results. This practice not only created a poor user experience but also led to a cluttered and unreadable text that confused visitors. However, as search engines evolved, they began to recognize the importance of context and relevancy. Google's algorithms introduced new metrics, focusing more on what users really wanted: quality content that answered their questions and provided value. This shift prompted webmasters to rethink their approach. Understanding that a good user experience, with clear navigation, quick loading times, and relevant content, would not only attract visitors but also keep them engaged, became essential. It encouraged website owners to focus on creating meaningful content that served real needs rather than just appealing to search engines.

By considering how SEO has transformed over time, we can gain insights into where it might be heading. The rise of artificial intelligence and machine learning is reshaping search engine algorithms again, emphasizing user intent and behavior more than ever. As small business owners and webmasters, it's critical to stay ahead of the curve and anticipate changes that prioritize the user experience. Understanding that search engines want to deliver the best possible results means that adapting to new tools and strategies—like voice search optimization and mobile-first indexing—is more important than ever. The digital landscape is ever-changing, and embracing these developments can give your website a competitive edge. One practical tip is to regularly audit your site's content and design to ensure it aligns with current best practices. This proactive approach can help you remain flexible and responsive to future trends in SEO.

1.3 Key Terminology Every Website Owner Should Know

Terms like search engine optimization, or SEO, have become buzzwords, but the meaning behind them is crucial for your website's visibility. Understanding these terms can make the journey less daunting and significantly enhance your ability to communicate with webmasters, digital marketers, or even your own understanding of the analytic data you encounter. Just as a chef needs to know the tools of their trade, understanding SEO terminology equips you with the knowledge to make informed decisions about your website's strategy. For instance, when you hear about "organic traffic," you'll know it refers to visitors who arrive at your site through unpaid search results, unlike paid ads. This understanding allows you to appreciate the value of developing content that not only resonates with your audience but also improves your ranking on search engines.

Backlinks are links from other websites that point to yours, and they serve as a vote of confidence in your content, signaling to search engines that your site is a credible source. The more high-quality backlinks you have, the more authoritative your site appears, and the better your chances are of climbing the rankings. SERP, or search engine results page, is where your website needs to shine. You may discover that being on the first page of a SERP significantly increases your chances of attracting visitors. Lastly, understanding CTR, or click-through rate, helps you gauge how effectively your website titles and descriptions attract attention. A high CTR indicates that people find your content enticing, while a low CTR may prompt you to reconsider your phrasing or focus. Keeping these terms at the forefront of your mind as you construct and refine your online presence will ultimately support the growth of your site and enhance its impact on your business.

Delving into SEO terminology isn't merely an academic exercise; it translates directly into actionable strategies that can benefit your website. Start engaging with these terms in your daily operations— monitor your backlinks to ensure quality, analyze your SERP standings regularly, and experiment with your meta descriptions to boost CTR. By doing so, you become an active participant in the ever-evolving digital space, ensuring that your website not only survives but thrives.

1.4 Future of SEO

The future of SEO is poised for dynamic transformation, heavily influenced by the growing capabilities of artificial intelligence. As algorithms become more sophisticated, they are beginning to mimic human understanding in remarkable ways. This evolution means that keywords will not just be searched for on a literal basis; instead, search engines will increasingly interpret the intent behind user queries. This shift necessitates an emphasis on quality content that resonates with audiences, rather than simply stuffing pages with keywords. Moreover, voice search optimization is becoming essential in this crowded digital landscape. With the proliferation of smart speakers and voice-assisted devices, more people are using conversational phrases when searching online. This trend signals a need for businesses to adapt, focusing on natural language queries and long-tail keywords. In this exciting future, success will hinge on the ability to anticipate and respond to these changes.

Staying informed about upcoming trends in SEO is more crucial than ever for maintaining a competitive edge online. The landscape is evolving rapidly, and those who remain in the dark risk losing significant ground to competitors who are willing to adapt. Regularly following trusted industry blogs, attending webinars, and participating in forums dedicated to SEO can provide valuable insights. Future trends might include a stronger focus on user experience, as search engines refine their metrics to consider site speed, mobile sensitivity, and overall navigation ease. Understanding these elements will empower small business owners and webmasters to adjust their strategies accordingly. It's not just about keeping up; it's about anticipating what comes next, ensuring your website remains relevant in a sea of constant change.

2. The Role of Content in SEO

2.1 Crafting High-Quality Content: Best Practices

When I write, I focus on connecting with readers on a personal level, bringing value through every word. It's not just about filling a page; it's about sparking interest and providing genuine information. Striking the right tone matters, as it can determine whether a visitor sticks around or quickly navigates away. I always aim to understand my target audience's needs and preferences. This understanding guides my writing, ensuring that the content is relevant and appealing. Using compelling narratives, relatable examples, and clear insights transforms an ordinary article into something remarkable. It becomes an experience rather than just information. The goal is to weave in facts, ideas, and stories that resonate deeply with readers, making them feel seen and heard.

One vital aspect is optimizing the structure of my content. I pay attention to headers and subheaders since they help organize the information and make it easier to digest. Keywords are also crucial, but I make sure to use them naturally within the text. Keyword stuffing can turn readers away and damage search visibility. I focus on a conversational style, mixed with strategic keywords, to keep things flowing smoothly. Another best practice is creating eye-catching meta descriptions and engaging titles. These elements act as the gateway for potential readers, so I invest time in making them enticing. Engaging multimedia, such as images or videos, can enrich the content and enhance user retention. I ensure that all visuals are high quality and relevant, as they complement the text and provide further value.

Ultimately, high-quality content should invite interaction. Encouraging comments or discussions can spark deeper insights and build a vibrant community around your website. By asking open-ended questions or providing unique call-to-actions, I give the audience a reason to engage. Remember, crafting high-quality content is not just about what you say but how you say it. A practical tip is to always keep your audience in mind, writing with their curiosity and needs at the forefront. When you align your content with your audience's interests while embracing SEO best practices, you pave the way for success, driving traffic and fostering loyalty.

2.2 The Importance of Keyword Research

Understanding what your audience is searching for is essential in shaping a successful content strategy. Keyword research serves as the beacon that illuminates the path to creating relevant content. When I dive into keyword research, I find that it opens up a treasure trove of insights, allowing me to see the words and phrases that resonate with my audience. It's not just about numbers and statistics; it's about connecting with the hearts and minds of those who seek your products or services. Knowing what people are typing into search engines helps tailor my content to their specific needs and questions, making it not only more relevant but also more engaging. This targeted approach not only increases the chances of my content being discovered but also fosters a stronger relationship with my audience, as they see that I am addressing their concerns directly.

By prioritizing the right keywords, I have witnessed firsthand the significant impact on visibility and traffic to my website. The right keywords can act as a magnet, drawing in new visitors who are eager to find the solutions I provide. Focusing on these keywords gives me an edge in the crowded online space, letting my content shine through the noise. It's fascinating to analyze how even minor adjustments in keyword choices can lead to drastic changes in website performance. I often compare it to having the perfect shop window—when it's attractive and relevant, people can't help but stop and take a look. By honing in on specific keywords, I not only attract more visitors but also ensure that these visitors are genuinely interested in what I offer, leading to higher conversion rates and a thriving online presence. For anyone striving to enhance their website's performance, understanding and implementing effective keyword research is not just important; it's absolutely vital.

As you embark on your journey of keyword research, consider utilizing tools like Google Keyword Planner or SEMrush, which can provide valuable insights into keyword volume and competition.

Begin with broad topics that relate to your business and gradually narrow down to specific phrases or long-tail keywords. In doing so, you not only discover gaps in the market but also learn how to speak directly to your audience's needs. Continuous analysis and refinement of your chosen keywords will keep your content strategy aligned with changing search behaviors, ensuring that you remain engaged with your audience for years to come.

2.3 Optimizing Content for User Intent

When someone types a query into a search engine, they have a specific goal in mind. They might be looking for information, seeking to buy a product, or wanting to find a service. When I write content, I think about what the user is really after. Is the person searching for a best coffee maker wanting a comparison of products, or are they ready to buy and just looking for the best deal? Diving deep into these nuances not only helps in crafting relevant content but also draws a clear line between guesswork and precise targeting. By addressing various types of user intent—navigational, informational, transactional, and commercial—I'm able to create a richer, more engaging experience that speaks to what my audience truly seeks.

When I focus on what users actually want, it naturally translates into metrics that echo satisfaction. Users tend to spend more time on pages that resonate with their intent, which sends positive signals to search engines. Crafting content with the user in mind not only involves the right keywords but enriching the text with valuable insights, clear calls to action, and engaging visuals that complement the message. Over time, as I implement these strategies, I notice that my pages climb higher in search results, attracting more organic traffic. This is not just about short-term wins; when users find what they need, they are more likely to return, share the content, and even convert into loyal customers. A practical tip is to always include questions within your content that reflect common queries related to your topic, as this not only helps in aligning with user intent but also enhances the likelihood of appearing in featured snippets in search results.

3. Technical SEO: The Backbone of Your Website

3.1 Understanding Website Structure and Indexing

When visitors land on your site, the first thing they notice is how easy it is to navigate. If the layout is logical and intuitive, visitors are likely to stay longer, explore more pages, and possibly convert into customers. Think of your website like a well-organized store; when everything has its place, shoppers can find what they're looking for quickly and effortlessly. This organization helps search engines too. Just as visitors appreciate clarity, search engines rely on a solid website structure to crawl your pages efficiently. Clear navigation menus, proper use of headings, and well-defined categories help search engines understand the relationship between different pages. If your website is clean and organized, not only will users appreciate it, but you will also likely see a positive impact on your search engine rankings.

Indexing is the process by which search engines store and organize information from your website in their vast databases. When you create new content, you want to ensure that search engines can find and index it quickly. Various factors affect indexing, including the frequency of updates to your site and how often search engine bots crawl your pages. Using XML sitemaps can greatly assist in this regard, as they provide a roadmap for search engines, detailing which pages are the most important and how they relate to each other. Moreover, high-quality, relevant content combined with strategic use of keywords helps ensure that your pages appear in search results when potential customers are looking for what you offer. Creating a thoughtful site structure and actively managing your content is not just good for user experience; it's essential for reaching new audiences effectively.

3.2 The Importance of Mobile Optimization

With more users accessing websites via mobile devices, optimizing for mobile has become essential for SEO. When I look at the statistics, it's hard to ignore the fact that a significant portion of web traffic comes from smartphones and tablets. If your website isn't mobile-friendly, you risk alienating a large segment of potential customers. This means not only losing visitors but also precious sales. Google has made it clear that mobile optimization is a crucial ranking factor in their search algorithms. This shift toward mobile has transformed consumer behavior, as people now expect to navigate your site effortlessly on their handheld devices. What's more, a slow-loading, poorly displayed website can deter users in an instant. They want to find what they're looking for quickly and easily, and if they can't, they will likely bounce to a competitor's site that offers a better mobile experience. Therefore, investing in mobile optimization isn't just a good idea; it's necessary for staying competitive in today's digital market.

Responsive design plays a fundamental role in enhancing user experience and is a key factor in search engine rankings. I've witnessed firsthand how responsive design can transform a complicated user experience into something seamless and enjoyable. When a website adjusts its layout according to the screen size of the device being used, visitors are more likely to engage with the content rather than struggle with pinching and zooming. This aspect of design not only makes navigation easier but also enhances overall satisfaction. Google favors sites that provide a good user experience, and responsive design is a must-have for anyone looking to climb the search engine ladders. It ensures that your content is accessible and displays beautifully on any device, from a desktop to the latest smartphone. Furthermore, maintaining a single URL for both desktop and mobile users simplifies the sharing of links and improves the indexing of your site by search engines. Both users and search engines appreciate a website that is adaptable and user-centered, leading to higher engagement rates and, ultimately, better conversions.

Embracing mobile optimization and responsive design isn't just a trend; it's an indispensable part of running a successful online presence. The time to act is now. Ensuring your website is optimized for mobile devices will set you apart from competitors who may still rely on outdated web practices. I recommend you regularly test your site on various devices to ensure that it's performing optimally. There are many tools available that can help simulate mobile navigation or report mobile usability issues. Making these improvements today can lead to greater visibility in search results, a happier audience, and, as a result, increased revenue.

3.3 Speed Optimization: Techniques for a Faster Site

Think about the last time you visited a website that took ages to load; the frustration is unbearable. Now, imagine putting yourself in your visitors' shoes. They want to access your content quickly without delays. If your site lags, potential customers will likely bounce away, seeking faster alternatives. This not only affects user retention but also diminishes your search engine rankings. Google and other search engines prioritize sites that load quickly, viewing speed as a marker for quality. In essence, enhancing your page speed isn't just about keeping visitors happy; it's about positioning your site right in the crowded digital marketplace. The faster your site, the better your chances of converting visitors into loyal customers.

There are several methods you can adopt to achieve this. One of the most effective is optimizing images; large files can slow down your site drastically. Compress images without sacrificing quality, and consider using modern formats like WebP, which provide better compression. Another approach is minimizing HTTP requests; this can involve reducing the number of elements on your page or combining files like CSS and JavaScript. Utilizing browser caching is also a smart strategy, as it allows returning visitors to load your pages faster, utilizing stored resources instead of re-downloading them. Additionally, choosing a dependable hosting service that is optimized for speed can make a world of difference. By employing these techniques, you create a smoother experience for your visitors, ultimately leading to greater engagement and higher conversion rates. Remember, every second counts in user experience—implementing the right strategies today can lead to noticeable improvements tomorrow.

4. On-Page SEO Strategies

4.1 Effective Use of Meta Tags

Meta tags play a crucial role in the world of online visibility. These snippets of text provide essential information to search engines, helping them understand what your webpage is about. When properly utilized, meta tags can significantly influence click-through rates, ensuring that when your website appears in search results, it stands out amidst the competition. When users see well-crafted meta titles and descriptions, they are more likely to determine that the content is relevant to their queries, leading to increased traffic to your site. Essentially, meta tags serve as a bridge between your content and potential visitors, making it imperative to pay attention to how they are structured and presented.

Crafting compelling meta titles and descriptions requires a balance of creativity and strategy. Your title should not only include the main keywords relevant to your content but also evoke curiosity or a sense of urgency. For example, instead of simply naming an article "Best Small Business Strategies," a more engaging title could be "Unlock Your Small Business Potential with These Proven Strategies." This approach not only informs the user about the content but also entices them to click on it. Similarly, your meta description should expand on this idea, offering a brief but informative overview that highlights the benefits of reading the page. By including action verbs and a few well-chosen keywords, you can create a description that resonates with both users and search engines, leading to a higher likelihood of attracting clicks.

Remember, the character limit for meta titles is generally around 50-60 characters, while meta descriptions are best kept under 160 characters. This restriction might seem limiting, but it forces you to be concise and thoughtful with your wording. Before finalizing your meta tags, consider using tools like Google's Preview Tool to see how your tags will appear in search results. An effective tip for optimizing your meta tags is to include a call-to-action, prompting potential readers to take the next step, whether that's clicking to learn more, signing up for a newsletter, or making a purchase. Always keep in mind the importance of relevance and clarity, as these elements not only enhance user experience but also strengthen your site's overall SEO efforts.

4.2 Good, SEO Friendly Titles Writing

Crafting an attention-grabbing title is not just about catching someone's eye but also about convincing search engines that your content is relevant and worth displaying prominently. Search engines like Google aim to serve their users the best possible results, which means your title must align with both their search intent and the content of your page. Successful titles usually contain a blend of clarity and intrigue, ensuring that when users scan through search results, your title stands out as the most appealing option. Imagine the moment when someone sees your intriguing title amidst a sea of mundane alternatives; that click is the first victory in working toward your content's success. Therefore, understanding the dynamics of SEO-friendly titles directly contributes to enhancing your visibility online.

Start by thinking about the main topic of your content and the specific keywords it should rank for. Integrating these keywords into your title isn't merely about stuffing them in; rather, it's about weaving them seamlessly into a compelling narrative. Using tools like Google Keyword Planner can provide insights into what your audience is actively searching for, allowing you to refine your title's efficiency. Beyond the keywords, you can implement emotional triggers, questions, and numbers to draw readers in. For instance, a title that poses a question often invites curiosity, while one that includes a number promises structured and digestible information. The goal is to make the title not only informative but also engaging, sparking the reader's interest long enough to encourage them to click through to your content. Writing catchy titles is a blend of art and science, requiring continuous refinement and creativity to keep pace with changing trends and audience preferences.

As you refine your title-writing technique, remember to test different variations and analyze their performance. Tools such as A/B testing can be incredibly beneficial in this regard—you can experiment with two different titles to see which performs better. Tracking metrics such as click-through rates will provide valuable insights into how your audience responds to each title. A title might seem perfect in theory, but actual performance can reveal fascinating insights into your audience's preferences. By engaging in this ongoing process of tweaking and testing, you not only improve your title-writing skills but also enhance the overall effectiveness of your content strategy. Embracing this adaptability is key, for the digital landscape is ever-evolving, and your titles should evolve right along with it.

4.3 Header Tags: Guide To H1, H2 to H6 Heading Tags For SEO

When I first dived into the world of web development, I underestimated the power of header tags. I quickly learned that header tags are essential for giving your content a clear framework. The H1 tag acts as the title of your page, briefly summarizing the main topic you're covering, while H2 through H6 tags help outline subsections in a hierarchy. This structure not only helps users easily navigate through your content but also allows search engines to understand the context and relevance of your pages. By clearly outlining your topics and subtopics, you enhance user experience and increase the chances of your content being effectively indexed by search engines. In essence, a well-structured webpage can keep visitors engaged longer and reduce bounce rates.

Effective use of header tags doesn't just enhance readability; it also has a direct impact on your SEO strategy. Begin with a unique H1 tag that includes your primary keywords. It's crucial to make this first impression count, as search engines prioritize the H1 tag. Following up with H2 tags helps you break down your content into bite-sized sections that are easy to digest, while H3 tags can be used for additional layers of subtopics. Consistency is key; hence, following a logical structure while avoiding keyword stuffing will yield better results. Additionally, ensure that your header tags are not just decorative but functional, directing readers through your narrative smoothly. A practical tip is to maintain a hierarchy; if you use an H2, support it with H3 tags rather than jumping to an H4 or H6. This logical progression aids both user comprehension and SEO optimization, guiding readers through your story while keeping search engines informed about your content's structure.

4.4 Enhancing User Experience through Design

It's fascinating how the marriage of aesthetics and functionality can greatly influence not just customer satisfaction but also how well your site ranks in search engines. When users find a website easy to navigate, with clear pathways to the information they seek, they are likely to spend more time there. This engagement signals to search engines that your site is valuable, which can boost your SEO efforts. A clean, streamlined design minimizes distractions and creates a smooth flow from one section to another. You want users to feel at home on your website, as if they instinctively know where to click next. This sense of familiarity fosters trust, and when users trust your website, they're more inclined to return, engage further, or even make a purchase. Moreover, the use of mobile-responsive design cannot be underestimated; in today's mobile-first world, ensuring that your website looks great and performs well across all devices is essential for both user experience and SEO.

Engaging design is all about understanding your audience and making it as easy as possible for them to achieve their goals. Utilize visual hierarchy to guide your visitors' eyes to the most important elements on your pages—this involves manipulating size, color, and placement to draw attention. For instance, call-to-action buttons should stand out clearly from the rest of the content, encouraging users to take action. Integrating interactive elements, like quizzes or calculators, can also significantly enhance engagement. This not only keeps users interested but can also provide you with valuable data about their preferences and behaviors. In addition, regularly updating your content can keep your audience coming back for more, as fresh and relevant information is key to maintaining user interest. It's about creating a dynamic platform where users feel continuously connected and valued. Every design choice should be intentional, with the end user always in mind, creating a positive feedback loop that benefits both user experience and site performance.

Think about A/B testing different layouts or features to see what resonates best with your audience. Often, small adjustments can yield significant improvements in engagement and satisfaction. Prioritize usability, as a site that is easy to navigate often leads to higher conversion rates. Always be open to feedback and willing to tweak your design to better meet user needs. A well-designed website is one that evolves along with its users' preferences and behaviors, ensuring that it remains relevant and effective in the long run.

4.5 Internal Linking Strategies for Better Navigation

Internal links are an essential part of any website's structure. They help users navigate your site smoothly, guiding them from one page to another while ensuring they find the information they're looking for. Think of internal links as the signposts on the highway of your website. They allow users to move between related pages without feeling lost or overwhelmed. Beyond enhancing user experience, internal linking plays a crucial role in distributing page authority across your site. When you connect relevant content, you're essentially telling search engines which pages are important and how they relate to one another. As a result, a well-structured internal linking system not only aids navigation but also boosts the visibility of your content in search engine results.

Implementing strong internal linking strategies can greatly improve the overall SEO of your website. When search engines crawl your site, they rely heavily on internal links to discover and understand the relationships between different pages. A thoughtful internal linking strategy can help increase rankings for certain keywords, as search engines use these links to gauge the relevance and authority of each page. Moreover, proper internal linking can reduce bounce rates by encouraging visitors to explore more of your site rather than leaving after viewing just one page. It is crucial to analyze your content regularly and identify opportunities to link relevant pages.

By doing so, you enrich the visitor's experience, and at the same time, reinforce your pages' SEO potential.

So, here's a practical tip: make it a habit to include internal links naturally within your content. Use descriptive anchor text that tells the reader what they can expect when they click the link. For instance, instead of using "click here," try incorporating the page's topic directly into the anchor text, such as "learn more about our digital marketing services." This approach not only assists users in navigation but also provides added context to search engines. The clearer you are with your internal links, the better the navigation and SEO benefits you will reap.

5. Off-Page SEO: Building Authority

5.1 The Power of Backlinks and How to Acquire Them

When other reputable websites link to your site, they are essentially vouching for your content. This endorsement is significant in the eyes of search engines, as it reflects credibility and trustworthiness. Think of backlinks as votes of confidence. The more high-quality backlinks you have, the more search engines recognize your site as an authority in your niche. This can lead to higher rankings on search engine results pages (SERPs), driving organic traffic to your site. Moreover, backlinks can help you reach new audiences, as they provide pathways for users to discover your content through other sites. Establishing a solid backlink profile is not just about quantity; it's about quality. A single link from a respected and relevant source often holds more weight than dozens of spammy links. Ultimately, backlinks play a pivotal role in boosting your overall search engine optimization (SEO) efforts, which can be the difference between a website that thrives and one that struggles to gain visibility.

Learning effective strategies for acquiring high-quality backlinks to boost your SEO can be a game changer. One key approach is to create exceptional, valuable content that naturally encourages others to link to it. This often involves investing time into research, format, and presentation, producing guides, infographics, or comprehensive articles that provide value to your target audience. Another effective strategy is active outreach. This can involve emailing bloggers, journalists, or influencers in your industry, introducing them to your content, and suggesting they might find it useful for their audience. Offering guest posts is another fruitful tactic; by writing for other websites, you can include a link back to your site. It's important to focus on niche relevance when seeking backlinks, as links from sites within your industry carry more weight. Building relationships with fellow webmasters can also foster organic backlink opportunities. Networking through social media platforms and online communities, sharing insights, or collaborating on projects can lead to mutually beneficial linking arrangements.

To maximize your backlink acquisition efforts, consider utilizing tools that allow you to analyze your competitors' backlink profiles. Understanding where they earn their links can provide insights and opportunities for your own strategies. Also, focus on maintaining a diverse backlink profile. This means seeking links from a variety of sources, including blogs, forums, local business directories, and social media platforms. Remember, while automated link-building schemes may seem tempting, search engines are increasingly adept at identifying these tactics, and they can lead to penalties that stomp your progress. Authenticity in your backlink strategy is crucial. A proactive yet genuine approach in building relationships and creating valuable content will yield better long-term results. Always remember that building backlinks is not just about quick wins; it requires ongoing effort and strategy to cultivate an effective backlink strategy that fosters trust and authority in your niche. Cultivating a culture of collaboration within your digital ecosystem can also lead to increased visibility and growth, as supporting each other tends to create a win-win situation for all involved.

5.2 Harnessing Social Media for SEO

Social media can significantly amplify your content's reach and contribute positively to your SEO efforts. When I first started my website, I underestimated the influence that social media could have on my search engine rankings. By sharing my content on platforms like Facebook, Twitter, and Instagram, I found that I could drive a considerable amount of traffic back to my website. Each share or like acts as a signal to search engines that my content is valuable and worthy of attention. This increased exposure can lead not only to higher website traffic but also to more backlinks and engagement metrics, which are crucial for improving SEO. Engaging with your audience through comments and direct messages allows you to foster relationships and establish a brand presence, which can enhance your online reputation—a factor that search engines favor when determining rankings.

To leverage social platforms effectively, focus on creating compelling content that resonates with your audience. Regularly posting updates, behind-the-scenes looks, or even user-generated content can help sustain interest and interaction. I learned that using eye-catching visuals, videos, and engaging captions can encourage shares and comments, ultimately directing more visitors to my site. Additionally, using relevant hashtags can broaden the reach of your posts, allowing them to be discovered by users outside your immediate network. It's important to track which platforms bring the most traffic to your site so you can concentrate your efforts where they matter most. Incorporating social sharing buttons on your blog or website is another great strategy; it makes it easy for readers to share your content, creating organic growth and enhancing your visibility.

As you continue to integrate social media into your marketing strategy, remember the importance of consistency. Regular activity on your chosen platforms keeps your audience engaged and the conversation alive. Analyze your performance through insights and analytics to refine your approach continually. Social media is not just about posting once in a while; it's about building a community and interactive environment that contributes positively to your website's SEO. One practical tip is to schedule your posts using social media management tools, ensuring that you maintain a steady flow of content and engagement. This way, you maximize your visibility without overwhelming yourself.

5.3 The Role of Influencers in Brand Promotion

In today's digital landscape, consumers are looking for authentic connections with brands. Influencers have the power to bridge that gap. They often have established trust with their followers, and when they partner with a brand, it feels more like a recommendation from a friend than a traditional advertisement. This means your brand message can resonate on a deeper level with the audience. Moreover, when an influencer shares your product or service, it skyrockets your reach. Their followers are often engaged and interested in what the influencer promotes, which can lead to increased visibility for your brand. This credibility can translate into increased sales and a more loyal customer base, as people are more likely to support a brand that they see endorsed by someone they admire.

When influencers create content featuring your brand and share it on their platforms, they're not just promoting your products; they are also generating valuable backlinks to your website. These backlinks from reputable sources can significantly improve your site's search engine ranking. The process helps your site gain authority, making it more favorable to search engines. Additionally, influencer collaborations can drive considerable traffic to your website. As people engage with the influencer's content and click through to your site, you're likely to see an uptick in not just visitors but also potential customers. It's a win-win situation; you enhance your online presence while benefiting from the influencer's established audience.

Remember, when selecting an influencer to collaborate with, choose someone whose values align with your brand and who has an audience that fits your target market. Authenticity is key, as followers can easily spot when an endorsement feels disingenuous. Establishing a genuine partnership with the influencer will result in more impactful content that resonates with their audience. As you explore this exciting avenue of marketing, keep in mind that influencers can do more than just promote your brand; they can help tell your brand story in a way that is engaging, memorable, and effective.

6. Local SEO Strategies

6.1 Understanding Local Search Dynamics

If you're a small business owner, website operator, or webmaster, neglecting local SEO in your marketing strategy can lead to missed opportunities. Customers often seek services tailored to their location, and optimizing your website for local search can provide you with the competitive edge you need. When you enhance your online presence for local searches, you not only reach people who are more likely to become customers but also establish your brand within your community. While traditional SEO focuses on broader audiences, local SEO hones in on those individuals who are searching right in your neighborhood. This means using location-based keywords, creating localized content, and ensuring that your Google My Business listing is complete and accurate. Indeed, local SEO is not just about appearing in search results; it's about being the preferred choice in your immediate region.

Understanding how search engines prioritize local results involves recognizing several key factors. Search engines, particularly Google, look at a variety of signals to determine which businesses to display when someone searches for services within a specific area. These signals include the relevance of your website content to the searcher's query, the proximity of your business to their current location, and the prominence or local authority of your business within the community. By focusing on optimizing these aspects—like ensuring that your contact information is accurate and consistently formatted across the web or encouraging positive reviews from satisfied customers—you can enhance your local listing's visibility. Engaging in local link-building initiatives and participating in community-based events also help signal to search engines that you're a credible and established business in the area. Understanding these dynamics isn't just about improving search rankings; it's about connecting authentically with your audience and building relationships that drive growth.

One practical tip to get started on your local SEO journey is to conduct a local keyword search. Use tools like Google Keyword Planner or Ubersuggest to find out which terms people in your area are using when they're seeking services you provide. This little investment of time can inform you on how to mold your content, update website metadata, and create targeted ads. Additionally, consider integrating these keywords into your website's blog or article topic ideas to boost engagement and relevance, potentially translating to higher search visibility. Prioritizing local keywords will pave the way for more connections and more customers, contributing to your long-term success.

6.2 Optimizing Google My Business Listings

It serves as your digital storefront, offering essential information about your business, such as location, hours, and services, directly to potential customers searching online. When someone types in a query related to your offerings, your listing can appear prominently in the local search results, enhancing your chances of being discovered. To make the most of this valuable tool, it's essential to fill out all the necessary fields completely and accurately. Ignoring this aspect can lead to missed opportunities as potential customers may not find you or may find outdated information that could dissuade them from choosing your business over competitors. Making sure that the contact details, business hours, and website URLs are correct and up to date is crucial for maintaining the reliability and trustworthiness of your listing.

Start by regularly updating your profile with fresh photos showcasing your products, services, and the atmosphere of your business. High-quality visuals catch the eye and can communicate more than words ever could. Additionally, encourage customers to leave reviews on your Google My Business page. Positive reviews not only enhance your online reputation but also help improve your local search ranking. Engaging with reviews by responding to both positive and negative feedback shows prospective customers that you value their opinions and care about the customer experience. Don't forget to utilize the posts feature, where you can share updates, special offers, and events relevant to your business. This keeps your audience engaged and informed, turning potential customers into loyal ones. Finally, take advantage of the insights provided by Google My Business to track how customers interact with your listing. This data can provide invaluable information on how to optimize your listing even further, tailoring your approach to better meet the needs and interests of your audience.

6.3 Building Local Citations and Reviews

When potential customers search for services or products nearby, they often rely on the information they find online. A business's presence in various local directories or on review sites acts like a digital handshake; it's a signal that says, We're here, and we're legitimate. The more citations a business has, particularly those that list accurate and consistent information like the address, phone number, and business category, the more credible it appears. This consistency helps improve local search engine rankings, making it easier for new customers to discover you amidst the competition. Moreover, when local users see a flurry of positive reviews, it builds trust and encourages them to choose your business over others. Each glowing review acts as a beacon that draws in potential customers, reassuring them of the quality of service they can expect. Essentially, building citations and gathering positive reviews form the backbone of a trustworthy online reputation, crucial for attracting and retaining local clients.

One of the first steps is to claim and optimize your Google My Business listing. This platform not only serves as a primary citation but also allows you to share essential business information and photos, which can capture the attention of potential customers. Additionally, don't overlook the importance of local directories, such as Yelp, Bing Places, and industry-specific sites. Listing your business on multiple platforms ensures that diverse audiences can find you, increasing visibility and credibility. After you have established your citations, focus on creating an environment where customers feel inclined to leave positive feedback. Reach out personally through follow-up emails after a purchase, or ask satisfied customers in-person if they would be willing to help your business grow by sharing their experiences online. Incentivizing reviews with discounts for future purchases can also be effective, but always ensure that you encourage honest feedback, as authenticity is key in building long-term trust. Remember, the goal is to make customers feel valued and appreciated, turning their positive experiences into compelling reviews that act as persuasive endorsements for your business.

Explore various platforms where local citations and reviews can be established, seeking not only quantity but also quality. Engaging with your audience through social media can create informal channels for reviews as well, while actively responding to both positive and negative feedback shows that you value customer opinions. Responding promptly builds relationships, turning a simple review into a two-way conversation. Regularly monitoring your online presence will help you maintain accuracy in your business information across all platforms, which is crucial to your reputation and SEO efforts. Lastly, never underestimate the power of storytelling. Sharing customer success stories or testimonials on your website can complement the reviews you collect elsewhere, presenting a well-rounded narrative of your brand. This not only helps attract new customers but also fosters a community of loyal advocates who will continue to uplift your business. A consistent strategy for citations and reviews can effectively set the stage for your success in the local market.

7. Utilizing SEO Tools and Analytics

7.1 Overview of Popular SEO Tools

As a website owner or small business operator, embracing the right tools can not only simplify your workflow but significantly enhance your site's visibility. The digital landscape can be overwhelming, and with a plethora of SEO tools available, it becomes crucial to find those that cater specifically to your needs. Tools designed for keyword research, backlink analysis, and website audits can uncover opportunities and highlight areas for improvement. Understanding how to use these tools effectively can enable you to make data-driven decisions, optimize your content, and attract more visitors. Each tool often provides unique features that can help you analyze your competitors, track your rankings, and understand your audience better, making them invaluable assets in the quest for online success.

 For instance, Google Analytics stands out as an essential tool, offering insights into your website's traffic and user behavior. It helps you understand where your visitors come from and which pages keep them engaged. Another powerful tool is SEMrush, known for its extensive keyword research capabilities, allowing you to identify the best keywords for your niche and analyze your competitors' strategies. Similarly, Ahrefs offers robust backlink analysis features, which can clarify your link-building efforts and improve your overall SEO strategy. User-friendly interfaces and comprehensive guides make these tools accessible even if you're new to SEO. Ultimately, selecting the right set of tools should align with your specific goals, whether you aim to improve your site's ranking, enhance user experience, or drive conversion rates.

To maximize the benefits of these SEO tools, consider integrating them into your regular workflow. Regular check-ins with these platforms can provide ongoing insights rather than treating them as one-off solutions. Setting measurable goals based on the data gleaned from these tools helps in tracking your progress over time. Staying updated with industry trends, and leveraging the full suite of tools available can empower you to adapt your strategies dynamically. Remember, SEO is not just about picking the right keywords; it's about understanding your audience's needs and aligning your content accordingly. By continuously optimizing your website using these powerful tools, you can stay one step ahead of the competition and ensure your business grows steadily in the digital space.

7.2 How to Analyze Your Website's Performance

 When I first started my website, I underestimated the importance of consistently monitoring its performance. Over time, I realized that just creating great content was not enough. I needed to be proactive in understanding how my site was functioning and where it was falling short. Analyzing performance involves looking at various metrics like page load times, bounce rates, and user engagement levels. This ongoing evaluation not only reveals how well my website is performing but also highlights areas that need fine-tuning. If I noticed high bounce rates on specific pages, it was a clear signal to delve deeper and understand why visitors weren't sticking around. By leveraging tools like Google Analytics, I could pinpoint exact metrics and make data-driven decisions to enhance user experience and drive conversions.

Understanding analytics data can initially feel overwhelming, but breaking it down makes it manageable and insightful. I remember struggling with all the numbers at first until I grasped that I didn't need to track everything at once. Instead, I focused on key performance indicators (KPIs) that mattered most to my business goals. Metrics like unique visitors, session durations, and returning visitors became my priority. I employed analytics tools to set up dashboards that simplified the data, making it easy for me to visualize trends over time. Regularly reviewing these insights helped me adjust my marketing strategies, refine my content, and increase my site's overall effectiveness. Additionally, understanding user behavior—like what pages they visit or how they navigate the site—enabled me to create a more personalized experience for them. This not only improved engagement but also fostered loyalty.

As I continued to analyze my website's performance, I learned to take actionable steps based on the insights gained. For instance, if my analytics showed that a particular blog post was receiving significant traffic but had a high exit rate at the end, it indicated that the content wasn't leading visitors to the next step. This prompted me to add relevant links to other pages or encourage newsletter sign-ups at the end of the post. Small tweaks like this, based on data analysis, can lead to substantial improvements in overall site performance and user satisfaction. Setting a routine for performance checks, perhaps on a monthly basis, ensures that I stay updated with the evolving needs of my users and the dynamics of the digital landscape. Remember, the goal isn't just to collect data but to transform this information into actionable insights that can drive your website's growth.

7.3 Interpreting Data to Make SEO Decisions

It's enthralling to consider how much data we have at our fingertips today. Every click, every search, and every interaction on our websites tell a story. As website owners and small business managers, it's crucial to learn how to read this data, as it acts as both a compass and a map in navigating the complex terrain of search engine optimization. The beauty of data lies not only in the numbers themselves but in the insights we can derive from them. Metrics such as organic traffic, bounce rates, and keyword rankings provide invaluable clues about how well our website is performing. The direction we should take next becomes clearer when we analyze patterns and trends in this data. For example, if a particular blog post suddenly receives a surge in traffic, it might indicate that it resonates with the audience. By understanding this, we can create more content in that vein, effectively capitalizing on existing interest and potentially boosting our overall site engagement and rankings.

Understanding how to interpret data to refine your SEO approach continuously can transform your website into a well-oiled machine. Each piece of data adds color to the picture we're painting of our online presence. Whether it's identifying which keywords drive the most traffic or noticing a drop in rankings for a specific term, interpreting these signals can guide our decisions. I've found that employing tools like Google Analytics or Search Console is immensely helpful in tracking performance metrics. For instance, if I see that certain landing pages have high bounce rates, it may indicate that those pages lack the content users are seeking. In response, I could revise the pages to include more engaging content or improve the call-to-action to ensure users are directed to more relevant areas of my site. Additionally, segmenting data by demographics allows us to tailor our approach even further, ensuring that the content we produce resonates with our target audience. Ultimately, the iterative process of collecting, analyzing, and refining data empowers us to organically enhance our SEO strategies over time without resorting to gimmicks or shortcuts.

To effectively interpret data and make informed decisions, we must remain curious and open-minded. Don't just settle for surface-level insights; delve deeper into the data to uncover hidden opportunities. For instance, consider setting aside regular time slots each month to review your website's analytics. This could reveal shifts in user behavior or highlight aspects of your site that may need attention. Perhaps you might discover new keywords that are becoming increasingly relevant to your audience or realize that a particular channel is driving more traffic than others. These insights are gold. Use them to experiment with alternative approaches or pivot your content strategy entirely. Furthermore, remember that SEO is not a one-time effort; it's an ongoing journey. By continuously interpreting the data you collect, you not only adapt to changes in search engine algorithms but also to the evolving needs of your audience. This proactive stance will ensure that your website remains competitive, ultimately leading to sustained growth and success.

8. The Future of Voice Search and SEO

8.1 The Rise of Smart Speakers and Voice Assistants

As I navigate my day, I realize just how integrated these devices are in our lives, from the moment I wake up and ask my smart speaker for the weather to the times when I order groceries with just a few spoken words. This convenience not only changes how we interact with technology but also how consumers search for information and make purchasing decisions. For small business owners and webmasters like us, it's crucial to understand that voice search isn't merely an option anymore; it's a requisite. This shift indicates a demand for more natural language conversational queries. Instead of typing "best pizza near me," your potential customers are now more likely to say, "Where can I find the best pizza?" Such changes in behavior necessitate a rethink of SEO strategies, ensuring that our content answers these spoken queries effectively.

Voice assistants leverage complex algorithms that interpret natural language and provide results based on relevance, context, and user intent. I often explore how these systems analyze the spoken word and deliver precise, concise responses. This insight allows me to refine my approach to content creation, focusing on the types of questions users might pose and the everyday language they employ. By incorporating conversational keywords and phrases into website content, webmasters can increase the chances of appearing in voice search results. Moreover, it's essential to recognize the power of local search in voice inquiries. Most users expect immediate, localized results, so having an optimized Google Business Profile and using geo-targeted keywords can significantly bolster visibility. Adapting to these technologies not only improves user engagement but also strengthens brand presence, ensuring that when someone asks, your business is the answer they receive.

One practical tip that I've found tremendously beneficial is to frequently revisit and update the content on your website to keep it relevant. As language and search behavior evolve, so should your content. Incorporating a blog or a FAQ section that addresses common voice queries can establish your authority in your niche while also aligning with the trends of voice search. Engaging with customers through social media and other platforms to learn what queries or phrases they use can also provide valuable insights. Voice search is an exciting and rapidly growing field, and those who embrace these changes now will undoubtedly reap the benefits as we move further into this new digital landscape.

8.2 Adapting Content for Voice Search Queries

When I think about voice search, I imagine someone asking a question as if they were conversing with a friend. This informal style has a significant impact on how I create and organize my content. To reach voice search users, who typically rely on smart speakers or mobile devices, I focus on incorporating natural language into my content. That means writing in a way that mimics spoken language, utilizing contractions, and favoring a friendly, conversational tone. I pay attention to the types of questions my audience is likely to ask and structure my content to answer those directly. This often involves using headings that echo the phrasing of common queries or incorporating FAQs into the content. The idea is to anticipate the user's intent and provide clear, concise answers that can easily be read aloud by voice assistants.

One of the techniques that has proven effective for me is the emphasis on local SEO. Many voice searches are location-based, with users looking for the nearest service or product. I make sure to include relevant local keywords in my content while also claiming my business on Google My Business. Additionally, optimizing for long-tail keywords is vital. Since voice searches tend to be longer and more conversational than traditional typed queries, I prioritize phrases that people often say out loud. This not only helps me capture voice search traffic but also aligns well with the kind of content I create. I also focus on improving page load times and mobile responsiveness, given that most voice searches occur on mobile devices. Engaging multimedia content, like videos and visuals, further enriches the user experience, helping me maintain visibility and relevance in the ever-evolving landscape of search.

As I refine my approach, I keep in mind that voice search technology is continually advancing. It's essential to stay agile and adapt to new trends as they emerge. Incorporating schema markup can provide extra context to my content, helping search engines understand it better and improving my chances of appearing in voice search results. Ultimately, combining these strategies with consistent testing and monitoring allows me to give my audience the best possible answers to their queries. In this dynamic realm, committing to ongoing optimization will ensure that my content not only resonates with my audience but also elevates my online presence.

8.3 The Implications of Natural Language Processing

Natural language processing, or NLP, is radically changing how search engines interpret the queries we input. This technological advancement means that search engines are becoming increasingly sophisticated at understanding context, semantics, and even the intent behind what we type. Imagine is it like having a conversation where the other person truly understands what you mean, rather than just the words you say. As this capability grows, search engines no longer rely solely on keyword matching; they now consider the broader context of a user's query. For webmasters and small business owners, this shift presents an invaluable opportunity. By creating content that resonates with how people naturally express their thoughts, we can increase our chances of being recognized and valued by search algorithms. In practice, this means paying attention to the kinds of questions potential customers might ask and tailoring your content to not just include relevant keywords but to encapsulate the intent and thoughts behind those keywords.

Understanding the implications of NLP can significantly shape your content strategy, leading to better SEO results. When we embrace this new perspective, we move away from the old-school idea of stuffing as many keywords into our articles as possible. Instead, focusing on creating comprehensive, meaningful content that addresses users' needs will make our websites more attractive not just to search engines but to actual users looking for genuine answers. By using a conversational tone, addressing common questions head-on, and providing clear, informative responses, we can enhance user engagement while improving our visibility in search results. Ultimately, the better we can connect with our audience through our content, the more likely we are to cultivate loyalty and drive traffic to our websites.

9. AI and Automation in SEO

9.1 How AI is Transforming SEO

As a website owner, navigating the vast landscape of search engine optimization can often seem overwhelming. However, with the rise of artificial intelligence, there's been a significant shift in how we understand and implement effective SEO strategies. AI-driven tools can analyze vast amounts of data in real time, delivering insights that were previously hard to come by. This wealth of information allows us to identify user intent more accurately, spot trending keywords, and even predict future search behaviors. Imagine having a virtual assistant that can help you decode complex analytics, optimize your content for better keyword targeting, and even recommend structural changes to your website for improved performance. This level of automation not only saves time but also enables you to focus on creating high-quality content that truly resonates with your audience.

Exploring how AI can enhance your SEO strategies reveals a plethora of opportunities for improving performance. One of the most exciting aspects of AI in SEO is its ability to personalize user experiences. By leveraging machine learning and predictive analytics, AI can help you tailor content to meet the specific needs and preferences of your audience. For instance, tools that analyze user behavior can provide recommendations on what content is most likely to engage potential customers, allowing you to create targeted campaigns that yield better results. Additionally, AI can assist in link building by identifying high-authority websites that align with your niche, making your outreach efforts more efficient. While some may worry that AI will replace the human touch in SEO, the truth is that it complements our efforts by providing data-driven insights that empower our creative processes. Embracing these advancements in technology not only keeps you competitive in a crowded marketplace but also helps you craft a more strategic approach to online visibility.

As you integrate AI into your SEO approach, remember that the key is to use these advanced tools as a means of enhancing your understanding of your audience and your market. Focus on gathering insights through AI analytics, and let these insights inform your content strategies, keyword targeting, and overall digital marketing efforts. Practical tip: Start small by utilizing an AI-powered tool that analyzes your current content and SEO performance. Use it to identify gaps in your strategy, and let it guide you in refining your approach. By continuously iterating based on AI insights, you will not only optimize your website but also grow your online presence in meaningful ways.

9.2 Using Automation Tools for Efficient SEO Management

 As a website owner or small business operator, you often find yourself juggling various tasks, from content creation to social media management, while trying to keep your search engine optimization on point. This is where automation comes to the rescue. Imagine having the ability to track your website's performance metrics, analyze keywords, or post updates without having to do each task manually. Automation tools eliminate repetitive tasks, allowing you to dedicate more time to strategy and creativity. They help you stay organized by scheduling and managing content publishing, reporting on SEO performance, and even optimizing your website for better search results. By employing these advanced technologies, you can improve your overall efficiency and make informed decisions based on data without getting lost in the minutiae of daily operations. The time you save can be redirected toward developing your brand and improving customer engagement, which is vital for growing your business.

 For instance, tools like SEMrush or Ahrefs can monitor your site's health and keyword rankings, providing insightful reports that keep you in the loop about your search performance. They can alert you to any changes that may impact your visibility, ensuring you can react quickly to maintain your rankings. Additionally, content management systems like WordPress offer plugins such as Yoast SEO that automate many on-page optimization tasks, helping to improve your content's searchability without the need for extensive manual adjustments. Other tools, such as Moz or Rank Ranger, provide insights into backlink analysis and competitor SEO strategies, which can inform your planning and help you stay ahead in the competitive online landscape. By leveraging these automation solutions, you not only enhance your productivity but also ensure that your SEO strategies are grounded in real-time data and best practices.

Consider integrating these tools into your regular workflow to create a robust and responsive SEO strategy. With automation handling the bulk of your data gathering and analysis, you can focus on what truly matters—crafting valuable content that resonates with your audience. Remember to frequently review the performance reports generated by these tools, as they provide critical insights into what's working and what needs adjustment. Staying proactive with your SEO management can lead to better search rankings, more traffic, and ultimately, a healthier bottom line for your business.

9.3 Top 30 ChatGPT Prompts for SEO Professionals

As someone invested in the online landscape, I often find that the right questions lead to remarkable insights and innovative strategies. Integrating ChatGPT into my SEO toolkit has proven to be invaluable. These prompts can help refine keyword strategies, optimize content, and even generate engaging meta descriptions. By engaging with an AI, I'm able to brainstorm more effectively, exploring avenues I might not have considered. This technology allows me to free up brain space, focusing on creativity while letting the AI handle the heavy lifting of data analysis and organization.

Here is one great ChatGPT prompt for analyzing your or competitor website.

"Analyze the content of [website] and identify the primary and secondary keywords they are targeting."

Here are 30 powerful ChatGPT prompts for SEO professionals, covering keyword research, content strategy, technical SEO, and more.

Keyword Research & Strategy

"Generate a list of long-tail keywords related to [your niche] with low competition and high search volume."

"Provide keyword clustering ideas for [your topic] to optimize for semantic search."

"Analyze the intent behind the keyword '[keyword]' and suggest the best type of content to target it."

"Suggest 10 high-converting LSI (Latent Semantic Indexing) keywords for [main keyword]."

"Generate a list of potential featured snippet opportunities for '[keyword]' and how to optimize content for them."

SEO Content Optimization

"Write a fully SEO-optimized blog outline for '[topic]' using the best structure for search rankings."

"Provide an engaging SEO title and meta description for an article on '[topic]' with high CTR potential."

"Analyze the top-ranking pages for '[keyword]' and provide key takeaways for beating them in search results."

"Suggest 10 engaging blog topics related to '[industry]' that have high search demand."

"Provide a step-by-step guide on how to optimize a blog post for '[keyword]' with on-page SEO best practices."

Technical SEO

"Create a checklist for a complete technical SEO audit for an e-commerce website."

"Explain how to fix common Core Web Vitals issues, including CLS, FID, and LCP."

"List the top 10 most important SEO optimizations for improving crawlability and indexability."

"How can I optimize JavaScript-heavy websites for search engines while maintaining user experience?"

"Generate an XML sitemap structure optimized for an [industry] website."

Local SEO

"List 10 advanced strategies for optimizing a Google Business Profile for higher local rankings."

"Provide a template for a locally optimized landing page for '[city/service].'"

"Suggest ways to build high-quality local citations for an [industry] business."

"How can I optimize my website for 'near me' searches in [location]?"

"List the top 5 local SEO ranking factors for 2025 and how to optimize for them."

Link Building & Off-Page SEO

"Suggest 10 innovative white-hat link-building strategies for a new website in [industry]."

"Generate an outreach email template for acquiring backlinks from authoritative websites."

"How can I use HARO (Help a Reporter Out) to gain high-quality backlinks?"

"List the best guest blogging opportunities in the [industry] niche and how to pitch effectively."

"Analyze the backlink profile of '[competitor's website]' and suggest opportunities for outranking them."

Advanced SEO & AI Integration

"How can I use AI to automate SEO tasks like keyword research, content optimization, and reporting?"

"Suggest a workflow for integrating AI tools like ChatGPT and Google Search Console for better SEO insights."

"How can structured data (schema markup) be optimized for '[industry]' to improve search visibility?"

"Provide a guide on how to leverage Google Discover for more organic traffic."

"What are the most effective ways to use ChatGPT for generating SEO-friendly content at scale?"

For instance, asking ChatGPT for the top relevant keywords related to a niche can open the door to targeted content strategies that drive traffic. Moreover, if I seek to understand the competitive landscape, I can prompt it to analyze competitors' strategies, uncovering gaps in my approach. Another powerful tactic is generating variations of a blog post title designed to captivate search engine users. Each prompt strategically employed can spark new ideas, helping me stay ahead of trends and maintaining my website's relevance. As I interact with ChatGPT, I discover not just prompts that provide answers but also those that challenge my thinking, leading to a deeper understanding of my audience's needs and preferences.

Here are 15 powerful ChatGPT prompts for Keyword Research & Strategy to help SEO professionals find high-impact keywords, analyze competition, and create effective content strategies.

Keyword Discovery & Expansion

"Generate a list of long-tail keywords related to '[your niche/topic]' with low competition and high search volume."

"Provide 20 high-intent keywords for '[industry/product/service]' that can drive conversions."

"Suggest keyword variations for '[main keyword]' that target different stages of the buyer journey."

"Find low-competition keywords for a new website in the '[industry]' niche that can rank quickly."

"Generate a list of question-based keywords related to '[topic]' for featured snippets and voice search optimization."

Keyword Clustering & Intent Analysis

"Cluster the following keywords into logical topic groups to create pillar and cluster content: [list of keywords]."

"Analyze the search intent behind '[keyword]' and suggest the best type of content to target it."

"Provide a keyword mapping strategy for an e-commerce site selling '[product category]' to optimize site structure and rankings."

"Find semantic keywords related to '[main keyword]' to improve topical authority and content relevance."

"Suggest 10 transactional keywords for '[product/service]' that can generate sales or leads."

Competitive Analysis & Keyword Trends

"Analyze the top-ranking pages for '[keyword]' and provide insights on how to outrank them."

"Identify trending keywords in '[industry]' for the next 6 months and suggest content ideas."

"Find high-traffic keywords that '[competitor's website]' is ranking for and suggest strategies to compete."

"Suggest evergreen keywords in '[niche]' that can drive consistent long-term organic traffic."

"Analyze the SERP features for '[keyword]' and recommend optimizations to win featured snippets, People Also Ask, and local packs."

Employing these AI-generated prompts allows for a more nuanced approach to SEO. For example, I can ask for suggestions on optimizing an existing piece of content based on current SEO best practices, or I can seek advice on building backlinks that would fit well within my specific industry. Through this continuous dialogue with AI, I refine my SEO workflows and bolster my online presence. Remember, adapting to new technologies in SEO not only enhances efficiency but also opens pathways for creative exploration. Embrace these AI tools as a partner in your digital marketing journey, and witness how they can elevate your strategies to new heights.

9.4 The Ethical Considerations of AI in Digital Marketing

Understanding the ethical implications of AI usage is vital for responsible marketing. As a small business owner or webmaster, it's essential to recognize that while AI can enhance marketing strategies by automating tasks and analyzing data, it can also lead to unintended consequences if not used mindfully. For instance, algorithms trained on biased data can perpetuate stereotypes, affecting how certain groups view your brand. The ethical ramifications of using AI in digital marketing go beyond just compliance with regulations; they delve into the moral responsibilities we hold as marketers. It's our duty to ensure that the technology we employ genuinely serves our customers' interests while fostering trust and transparency. This requires being vigilant about what data is collected and how it influences our decisions and tactics. By prioritizing ethical considerations, we can create marketing strategies that do not just rely on advanced technology but also honor the relationship we share with our audience.

Reflecting on how to navigate AI in a way that is respectful and beneficial to users brings us to the heart of the matter. It's easy to get caught up in the excitement of AI capabilities and the data insights it can provide. However, the essence of successful digital marketing lies in genuine connection and user satisfaction. By adopting an ethical approach, we can ensure that our AI initiatives align with these values. For example, when using AI for personalized recommendations, it's crucial to maintain a balance between customization and privacy. Communicating openly with users about how their data is utilized can help alleviate privacy concerns and enhance their trust in our brand. Furthermore, we can prioritize user experience over mere conversion rates. By focusing on providing real value and fostering authentic engagement, we can harness AI not just as a tool for profit but as a means of enriching the lives of those we serve. This mindful practice creates a more loyal customer base and builds a brand reputation grounded in respect and integrity.

As you explore the integration of AI tools within your digital marketing strategy, consider implementing a user-first perspective in all your AI-driven initiatives. Evaluate the ethical implications of your data collection methods and commit to making transparent and responsible choices. Regularly reassess your strategies to ensure that they adapt to changing societal expectations and technological advancements. By leading with ethics in mind, you create a sustainable path forward that fosters trust and loyalty with your audience, ultimately setting your business apart in a crowded marketplace.

10. Crafting an Effective SEO Strategy

10.1 Setting Clear SEO Goals for Your Business

When I first ventured into the world of SEO, I quickly realized that without defined objectives, everything I did felt like tossing spaghetti at the wall, hoping something would stick. I found myself overwhelmed by the myriad of metrics available; keyword rankings, organic traffic, backlinks, and conversions can easily cloud your focus. I learned that by setting specific, measurable goals, I could better understand where my strengths lay and where I needed to improve. For instance, instead of simply aiming to get more traffic, I crafted a goal like increase organic traffic by 30% in six months. This simple yet powerful shift in perspective helped me to channel my efforts effectively and stay motivated. Break down your SEO efforts into manageable accomplishments, and you'll find it much easier to monitor your return on investment (ROI) and make informed decisions for future strategies.

Learning how to set goals that align with your overall business objectives can transform the way you approach SEO. It's important to sit down and reflect on what your business truly seeks to achieve. Are you looking to boost sales, enhance brand awareness, or foster customer loyalty? Mapping out your SEO goals to your business vision provides clarity and purpose to your digital marketing endeavors. I recall a time when I was working with a small retail business aiming to expand its online presence. By aligning their SEO goals with their overarching mission of engaging customers and driving sales, we created a targeted approach. We focused on optimizing product pages for high-converting keywords and producing valuable content that addressed customer pain points. As a result, not only did website traffic improve, but so did engagement and sales, all because our SEO strategies were directly tied to the business's core objectives.

In crafting your goals, consider using the SMART criteria: Specific, Measurable, Achievable, Relevant, and Time-bound. It's a framework that can help turn vague ambitions into concrete plans. For example, instead of the broad goal of improving search rankings, think like a strategist—Increase the ranking of our primary service page from the 5th to the 1st position in Google for the keyword 'best local plumber' within the next three months. Such specificity brings clarity and urgency, ensuring that every action you take in your SEO efforts is aligned with achieving desired outcomes. Ultimately, remember that setting clear goals is more than a planning exercise. It fuels your passion, ensures accountability, and brings purpose to your daily efforts, increasing momentum on the path to achieving remarkable results. If you adopt this approach, you'll not only navigate the complexities of SEO better but will also pave the way for sustained success.

10.2 Developing a Roadmap for Success

I have always found that having a clear plan in place can make the daunting world of search engine optimization feel much more manageable. It's like setting out on a road trip without a map; you may eventually reach your destination, but you'll probably encounter a lot of wrong turns and delays along the way. A well-thought-out SEO roadmap provides direction, helping to prioritize tasks and establish a timeline for achieving your goals. It keeps you focused on performance metrics that matter while allowing you to adapt to changes in the digital landscape. Whenever I craft an SEO roadmap, I start by assessing the current state of my website. This assessment helps identify strengths to build upon and weaknesses that need addressing. The key is to be honest and thorough during this review, as all the advancements hinge upon this initial understanding.

Exploring the key components of an effective SEO roadmap reveals more than just a checklist; it's a framework for continuous growth. Key components include keyword research, which should be the backbone of your strategy, guiding content creation and optimization. Understanding your target audience's search intent allows you to develop content that resonates with them. Equally important is site structure and technical SEO, ensuring that your website is user-friendly and easily accessible to search engines. Tracking and analyzing performance with tools like Google Analytics is a must, as it enables you to get real-time feedback on what's working and what isn't. The road to success also includes regular updates; the digital landscape is always evolving, and staying relevant means updating your strategy as trends shift. All these elements come together to create a map that not only routes you to higher rankings but also fosters genuine engagement with your audience.

As I've navigated through these processes, one practical tip that has served me well is to remain flexible. While the roadmap is a crucial guide, the ability to pivot when necessary can save you time and effort. If a particular keyword isn't performing as expected or a new trend emerges, don't hesitate to adjust your strategy. Incorporating regular check-ins into your roadmap allows you to reflect on your progress and make informed decisions about your next steps. SEO is a marathon, not a sprint, and keeping your roadmap dynamic ensures that you're equipped to adapt and thrive continuously.

10.3 Regularly Updating Your SEO Strategy

The online landscape is a dynamic one, constantly influenced by new technologies, shifting consumer behaviors, and changes in search engine algorithms. As a website owner, small business operator, or webmaster, it's crucial to stay ahead of these changes by continuously evaluating and refining your SEO practices. This involves not just making sporadic adjustments but integrating a rhythm of regular assessments into your routine. By doing so, you can identify what's working and what isn't, capitalizing on trends while avoiding tactics that may no longer yield results. It's like tending to a garden; you can't just plant seeds and walk away. You need to nourish, prune, and sometimes even plant new flowers to ensure that your garden thrives amidst the changing seasons.

One worthwhile practice is setting a schedule for regular reviews of your SEO metrics. This could be monthly or quarterly, depending on how often your industry changes. Use tools like Google Analytics or SEMrush to evaluate which keywords are driving traffic, how your rankings have shifted, and what content resonates most with your audience. Additionally, don't shy away from experimenting with new keywords or updated content formats, like videos or podcasts, as consumer preferences evolve. Engage with your audience, gather feedback, and look for patterns in their behaviors that may impact search queries. It's also beneficial to follow industry blogs and forums to keep your finger on the pulse of the latest SEO trends, innovations, and algorithm updates. Adaptability is key in SEO, so embracing a mindset of flexibility and curiosity will empower you to pivot strategies as necessary.

In the realm of SEO, consistency and awareness can help you stay relevant and ahead of competitors. Consider implementing an SEO checklist that you can refer to during each review cycle. This checklist will serve as a guide to ensure all vital aspects, such as meta titles, headings, backlinks, and content quality, are being monitored and updated. And don't forget the importance of mobile optimization, as an increasing number of users now search primarily from their mobile devices. Keeping your website responsive to different devices is not just a trend but a necessity in today's digital world. By fostering a proactive approach and dedicating time to continually refine your SEO strategy, you can build a resilient online presence that adapts to changes and thrives.

11. Mobile-First Indexing and Its Impact

11.1 Understanding Mobile-First Indexing

This shift marks a significant change in how search engines assess the content of websites. Traditionally, Google would look at the desktop version of a site first, but now it evaluates the mobile version instead. For you as a website owner or small business person, this means that if your site is not optimized for mobile, you could be losing potential customers. With more people accessing the internet on their smartphones, ensuring that your mobile site is functional and appealing is no longer optional; it is essential for maintaining visibility in search results.

Mobile-first indexing emphasizes the importance of having a responsive design and fast loading times. You need to ensure that your website provides a seamless experience for mobile users, as this directly impacts your search rankings. Look into aspects such as text size, image scaling, and navigation ease on smaller screens. Google's algorithms are designed to reward sites that prioritize these experiences, so if your website looks and functions well on a mobile device, you're more likely to rank higher in search results. Taking a proactive approach now not only prepares your website for the future but also enhances the overall user experience for mobile visitors.

A practical tip to keep in mind is to regularly test your site's performance on various mobile devices. Tools like Google's Mobile-Friendly Test can provide insights into how your site appears and functions on mobile screens. This not only helps you stay ahead in search rankings but also boosts customer satisfaction by ensuring that visitors find what they need quickly and easily, regardless of the device they are using. In a world that increasingly values mobile accessibility, making these adjustments will position your website for success.

11.2 Best Practices for Mobile Optimization

Implementing mobile optimization techniques can significantly enhance both user experience and search engine optimization (SEO). Today, more individuals access the internet through mobile devices than ever before, rendering a mobile-optimized website not just advantageous but essential. A site that is accessible and easy to navigate on a smartphone or tablet can lead to longer visit durations, reduced bounce rates, and higher conversion rates. The mobile experience should be seamless; this means that your website must load quickly with responsive design that adjusts smoothly to different screen sizes. Focusing on the user journey is crucial here because the easier you make it for your visitors to find what they need on their mobile devices, the more likely they are to engage fully with your content or products. Beyond user satisfaction, search engines like Google reward mobile-friendly sites with better rankings, making optimization a strategy that addresses both the visitor and the algorithm.

Critical best practices for ensuring your site performs well on mobile devices include adopting a responsive design, which allows your layout to adapt automatically to various screen sizes. This flexibility prevents the need for users to zoom in or scroll horizontally. Loading speed is another essential component; if your site takes too long to load, users will likely abandon it for a competitor's site. To enhance speed, consider optimizing images, leveraging browser caching, and minimizing JavaScript and CSS. Furthermore, streamline your navigation by using a mobile-friendly menu that makes it simple for visitors to access different sections of your site without fuss. Think about touch usability, ensuring buttons and links are large enough and spaced adequately to prevent accidental clicks. Test your site rigorously across multiple devices and platforms to address any potential issues that could detract from the mobile user experience.

In addition to these techniques, keeping content concise and easy to digest on mobile is fundamental. Visitors often appreciate a quick read that gets straight to the point without unnecessary fluff. Break down your content with clear headings and short paragraphs, making it easier to scan. Integrating larger fonts ensures readability without needing to zoom in. Remember that local SEO practices also play a significant role in mobile optimization. Most mobile searches are local, so providing your audience with pertinent location-based information can greatly benefit your visibility. Regularly revisiting and updating your mobile strategy is vital in staying current with ongoing technological advancements and evolving user habits. To ensure continuous improvement, gather analytics to measure mobile performance and user engagement metrics. This will give you deeper insight into areas that may need adjustment or enhancement, ultimately leading to a better mobile experience for your visitors.

11.3 Tools to Test Mobile Friendliness

With the rapid growth in mobile browsing, ensuring that your website performs well on smartphones and tablets is crucial. These tools allow you to analyze various aspects of your site, including load speed, responsiveness, and overall usability. One of the first things you might notice when using these tools is the emphasis on user experience. A mobile-friendly site not only fits nicely on smaller screens but also enables seamless navigation; this enhances your visitors' experiences and can lead to increased engagement and conversions. Being proactive in testing keeps your website aligned with the expectations of today's users and helps ensure that you're not missing out on potential traffic or sales due to a subpar mobile experience.

There are several popular options available that cater to different needs. For instance, Google's Mobile-Friendly Test allows you to enter your website URL and provides you with a detailed analysis on how well your site works on mobile devices. It highlights specific issues and gives suggestions for improvement. Similarly, tools like GTmetrix and Pingdom focus on testing load times and provide insights on optimizing your site's speed, which can significantly impact mobile users who often expect instant access to content. The responsive design checker is another helpful tool; it allows you to visualize how your website looks on different screen sizes, ensuring that your design remains consistent and effective across devices. By leveraging these tools, you can gain critical insights into your mobile site's performance and implement necessary changes. Remember, making improvements based on these insights can greatly enhance user satisfaction and boost your site's visibility in search results.

12. The Importance of User Experience (UX) in SEO

12.1 How UX Impacts SEO Rankings

When users find what they are looking for quickly and enjoyably, they are more likely to stay on your site longer. This reduced bounce rate signals search engines that your content is relevant and valuable, which can lead to improved rankings. Think of it this way: if visitors are happy with their experience on your site, they're more likely to trust it and return, which boosts your authority over time. Furthermore, engagement metrics such as clicks, time spent on page, and interactions with elements of your site all contribute to the algorithmic love that search engines have for your content. Ultimately, an outstanding user experience helps cultivate a positive perception of your site, making it more favorable in the eyes of search engines.

Speed is often the first element to consider; a slow-loading website frustrates users and can quickly lead them to click away. Search engines take this into account, as they aim to provide users with the best outcomes. Similarly, mobile-friendliness is crucial nowadays, especially with more users browsing on their phones than ever before. Google and other search engines are increasingly prioritizing mobile-optimized sites, understanding that a seamless experience across devices enhances user satisfaction. Navigation and site structure also play essential roles; if visitors can't find what they need, they will leave, and those exit rates negatively impact your SEO. Additionally, elements like readable fonts, strategic use of whitespace, and compelling visuals all contribute to how users perceive and interact with your site. All of these factors intertwine and reinforce one another, creating an environment where improving user experience naturally leads to better SEO performance.

Keep in mind that enhancing user experience isn't just about attraction; it's also about retention. Regularly evaluating usability through metrics and user feedback can help you identify pain points where visitors might be struggling. Conducting A/B testing can help you determine which designs work best and how small changes can lead to significant improvements in both user satisfaction and search rankings. Always remember, every aspect of your website's UX plays a role in SEO; by creating a coherent, welcoming, and efficient environment for users, you're not only serving your audience better but also paving the way for climbing higher in search results.

12.2 Designing for the User Journey

Every time a user interacts with your website, they embark on a journey. From the moment they land on your page to when they make a purchase or seek information, every click, scroll, and interaction reveals their state of mind. Understanding this journey is crucial for creating a meaningful experience. By placing empathy at the center of your design process, you can anticipate user needs and frustrations. This proactive approach allows you to craft a website that not only captivates but also retains users, creating a sense of loyalty that's invaluable for small businesses.

A seamless user experience doesn't just happen; it requires careful planning and attention to detail. Start by mapping the user journey from the first point of contact to the end of their experience on your site. Identify potential pain points—areas where users might feel lost or frustrated—and implement solutions that lead them smoothly from one stage to the next. Utilize analytics tools to gain insights into user behavior; these metrics help you pinpoint where users thrive and where they struggle. For instance, if users frequently abandon their carts, it signals an issue in the checkout process that must be addressed. Focus on clarity and simplicity throughout your design to facilitate ease of navigation, ensuring that users find exactly what they're looking for without unnecessary complications. Remember, a user-centric approach translates to better retention rates and increased satisfaction.

Creating an effective user journey is about continuous improvement and adaptation. Regularly gather feedback from users and be open to making adjustments based on their experiences. Conduct surveys, usability tests, or simply ask users for their thoughts after key interactions. This not only shows users that their opinions matter but provides invaluable insights into how your website can evolve to meet their expectations. A well-designed user journey is a living entity, and by treating it as such, you can cultivate an engaging online presence that keeps users coming back. A practical tip to enhance your user journey is to personalize experiences based on previous interactions. Tailor content and recommendations to users' needs; even subtle changes can lead to a significant impact on user satisfaction and, ultimately, your bottom line.

12.3 Measuring User Engagement Metrics

These metrics reveal how users are interacting with your content, helping you understand what resonates with them and what doesn't. When I first started tracking engagement, I discovered that it's not just about the number of visitors; it's about what those visitors do while they are on your site. For instance, tracking metrics such as bounce rates, time spent on the page, and pages per session can give you a clearer picture of user engagement. A high bounce rate might indicate that visitors aren't finding what they expected, while longer time spent on a page often means that your content is hitting the mark. Tools like Google Analytics make it incredibly easy to gather this data, but the real challenge lies in analyzing it and understanding the story behind the numbers.

It's important to establish clear goals for your website beforehand; without them, it can be difficult to interpret your metrics effectively. When defining your goals, consider what you want your visitors to accomplish on your site, whether it's making a purchase, signing up for a newsletter, or simply finding information. Regularly reviewing analytics helps ensure you stay aligned with these goals. In addition, segmenting your visitors can provide even deeper insights. By breaking down your data according to the source of traffic—such as organic search, social media, or email campaigns—you can compare how different audiences engage with your content and what pathways lead to conversions. Lastly, always remember that context is key. Combining your engagement metrics with user feedback or surveys can help you make informed decisions about updates and changes needed to boost engagement further.

13. Navigating Algorithm Updates

13.1 Understanding Google's Algorithm Changes

Each time Google rolls out an update, the way your website is evaluated can shift dramatically. This means that what may have worked yesterday in terms of search engine optimization could become less effective or even detrimental today. It's not just about keywords anymore; it's about the overall quality of your content, user experience, site speed, mobile responsiveness, and even the way users interact with your site. I've seen firsthand how a single algorithm update can send a website tumbling down the search results or launch it into the top spots. For instance, after the introduction of the Panda update, many thin-content sites found themselves struggling. Understanding these changes is crucial if you want to maintain or improve your site's visibility online.

Keeping an eye on what these updates entail and how they affect your website is vital for staying relevant. Google usually provides a bit of insight into what their updates focus on, often steering us towards prioritizing user intent, content relevancy, and overall website authority. By interpreting these signals, I started to pivot my SEO strategies. Instead of just pumping out content with specific keywords, I focused more on delivering thorough, valuable, and engaging content. Utilizing analytics tools has also helped track how my site performs with each change, allowing me to make informed tweaks. For small business owners, staying ahead of these changes can mean the difference between thriving online and fading into obscurity. Adapting to Google's algorithm changes isn't optional; it's a necessity to ensure your website not only reaches your target audience but also provides them with what they are truly looking for.

13.2 How to Adapt to Major Updates

 I've learned through experience that staying ahead of the game is the best way to protect your website or business from the potential fallout of algorithm changes. These updates can arrive unexpectedly, altering how search engines rank pages and often leaving many website owners scrambling to adjust. When I faced a significant update, I quickly realized that the key to weathering the storm was to constantly monitor official communications from search engines, as well as industry news and trends. By doing this, I was able to have a sense of what changes might affect my site. I also understood the importance of keeping my content relevant and high-quality, making sure it served the needs of my audience rather than just focusing on ranking high on search results. This proactive approach didn't just help me bounce back; it made my site more resilient to future changes.

Learning effective strategies to adapt your SEO efforts following updates is equally crucial. After an update, I found myself revisiting the fundamentals of my SEO strategy to ensure they aligned with best practices. The first step was to analyze the changes that had been made and how they might affect my current approach. I started by assessing my website's performance metrics, using tools that track key indicators like organic traffic and engagement time. By identifying the specific areas that had dropped in rankings, I could focus my efforts effectively. It was also valuable to engage with the community of fellow website owners and SEO experts to gather insights and share experiences. Collaboration can often reveal strategies that I wouldn't have considered on my own. Importantly, I also focused on optimizing my website for user experience. This meant enhancing site speed, improving mobile responsiveness, and ensuring intuitive navigation. All these steps not only helped in adapting to the latest algorithm changes but also increased user satisfaction, which is an essential factor in maintaining good rankings moving forward.

In the face of updates, a proactive mindset can make all the difference. Always be ready to embrace change rather than resist it. Remember, your adaptability and willingness to improve will not only shield your website from negative impacts but also strengthen it for the long haul. Regularly update your content and keep testing different strategies. One invaluable tip I've found is to create a system for monitoring SEO changes and trends. A dedicated schedule for reviewing your analytics and SEO performance can keep you in the loop and allow you to make timely adjustments. The more informed you are, the better prepared you will be when the next update comes around.

13.3 Keeping Up with Future Trends

The digital landscape shifts rapidly, often faster than one can anticipate. This dynamism can feel overwhelming, especially for small business owners or webmasters trying to keep their websites relevant. I often find myself immersed in various resources, from authoritative blogs and newsletters to podcasts and webinars, each providing insights and updates on the latest practices and changes in search algorithms. Google, for instance, seems to unveil updates at a breakneck pace, and understanding these changes is vital. Regularly engaging with SEO communities, participating in forums, and following industry leaders on social media can give you the edge required to adapt swiftly. By remaining curious and proactive, I not only equip myself with knowledge but also build a network of like-minded professionals who can offer support and share best practices.

Exploring practices for keeping up with the dynamic world of digital marketing becomes a practice of ongoing learning. One effective approach I've found is to allocate time each week to review new trends and tools. Whether it's testing out SEO plugins, experimenting with content formats like video or podcasts, or evaluating new keywords research methods, hands-on learning allows me to better grasp how these trends might fit into my overall strategy. Networking with colleagues and attending webinars can also provide fresh perspectives, often shedding light on innovative strategies that have worked for others. I focus on integrating these lessons into my daily operations, continuously refining my techniques and keeping my website competitive. One straightforward idea is to sign up for a few reputable newsletters; they often distill complex trends into digestible segments that can inspire actionable changes on your site.

Furthermore, tracking the performance of your website analytics allows you to connect the dots between emerging trends and your own results. By regularly analyzing metrics such as organic traffic, bounce rates, and user engagement, I can identify which strategies are resonating with my audience and which need tweaking. Being able to pivot my strategy based on real data rather than guesswork significantly boosts my confidence and effectiveness. It's important to remember that staying ahead is not merely about reacting to changes, but about anticipating them. Therefore, being adventurous with your strategies, testing different content styles, or even embracing platforms that are gaining popularity can open new avenues for reaching your target audience. Stay agile, be observant, and let your passion for your work fuel your journey in adapting to the future of digital marketing.

14. SEO Myths and Misconceptions

14.1 Debunking Common SEO Myths

As I dove deeper into the world of search engine optimization, I quickly realized that misconceptions were rampant. One of the most common myths is the belief that simply stuffing keywords into your content will boost your rankings. This outdated practice not only provides a poor experience for readers but can also trigger search engine penalties. Instead, the focus should be on creating valuable, relevant content that naturally incorporates keywords while addressing the needs and interests of your audience. Quality content engages users, prompting them to stay longer on your site, reducing bounce rates, and signaling to search engines that your site is trustworthy.

For instance, many people think that having a high volume of backlinks is the ultimate key to SEO success. While backlinks from reputable sites are important, the quality of those links outweighs the quantity. A single link from a well-respected site can be far more beneficial than ten links from lesser-known sources. Additionally, some believe that SEO is a set-it-and-forget-it strategy. In reality, the landscape of SEO is constantly evolving due to changes in algorithms and user behavior. Regularly updating your content, monitoring analytic metrics, and staying informed about industry trends are essential to maintaining strong SEO performance. By focusing on quality, relevance, and a proactive approach, you can navigate past these myths and develop effective SEO strategies that truly work for your website.

As you work on your SEO strategies, remember that debunking these myths is just the first step. The real work lies in implementing an approach that prioritizes user experience and engagement. Utilizing tools to analyze your website's performance can offer insights into what is working and what might need adjustment. Regularly review your content, check for technical issues, and ensure that you are providing your audience with valuable information that keeps them coming back. Adopting a mindset focused on continuous improvement rather than a one-time fix will pave the way for long-term success in the ever-changing digital landscape.

14.2 The Truth About Keyword Stuffing

In the early days of the internet, some website owners believed that cramming a web page with as many keywords as possible would guarantee higher rankings in search engine results. They would repeat phrases endlessly, often to the point where the content became unreadable and lost all value to the user. Search engines quickly caught on to this tactic. They developed sophisticated algorithms designed to improve user experience by prioritizing high-quality content over artificially optimized web pages. Today, keyword stuffing can lead to penalties that severely affect your website's visibility. If your content appears spammy or irrelevant, search engines may decrease your rankings or even remove your site from search results entirely. It's essential to move away from this old notion and understand that quality, relevance, and readability matter far more than sheer keyword frequency.

Today's approach to SEO emphasizes creating valuable content that genuinely serves your audience's needs. Instead of fixating on single keywords, focus on context, user intent, and the topics that surround your primary themes. For instance, rather than stuffing your article with the same keyword over and over, aim to cover various aspects of your topic naturally. This could mean engaging with related questions, utilizing synonyms, or exploring particular angles that your audience might be interested in. By embracing this holistic approach, you not only make your writing more pleasant and informative but also help search engines understand the nuanced nature of your content. A well-structured article that provides meaningful insights often ranks higher and garners more organic traffic. Remember, your primary goal should always be to provide exceptional value for readers; search engines will reward efforts that enhance user experience.

When crafting your content, think about how you can meet the needs of your audience without sacrificing the quality of your writing. Focus on comprehensive responses that address specific queries related to your niche. Use tools like keyword research and analytics to identify relevant topics, but let these tools guide you rather than dictate your content. It's about finding a balance, incorporating keywords naturally into coherent, useful, and entertaining prose. Always ask yourself: does this content help the reader? If you stay committed to providing value and authentic experiences, you'll likely see positive results in your rankings and engagement over time. Consider conducting regular audits of your content to ensure it aligns with current SEO best practices, and update where necessary to keep everything relevant and impactful.

14.3 Understanding the Role of Domain Age

It's easy to think that an older domain automatically means better rankings, perhaps because it has had more time to build authority and trust. However, there are many dimensions to SEO that require our attention. For example, domain age contributes to your website's credibility in the eyes of search engines, but factors like content quality, audience engagement, backlinks, and site speed are often far more critical. An older domain without fresh, relevant content may not perform as well as a newer domain that actively publishes valuable information and engages its audience. I've seen many websites with youthful domains achieve remarkable successes by prioritizing quality content and effective marketing over merely leaning on the age of their URLs. So, understanding that while domain age can aid your efforts, it shouldn't overshadow other needed strategies is crucial for anyone running a website or small business.

Learning how to focus on more impactful SEO strategies beyond just domain age is essential for any webmaster. Quality content is key; crafting engaging and informative articles that resonate with your audience is one of the best ways to improve your site's visibility and authority. Creating a responsive and user-friendly website also plays a significant role in retaining visitors, thus signaling to search engines that your site is worth promoting. Additionally, building quality backlinks from reputable sources can have a profound effect on improving your position in search results. Social signals, such as shares and likes, can promote your content organically and help establish your brand even further. Prioritize your marketing efforts— whether through social media, email campaigns, or collaborations with influencers—to broaden your reach. Remember that a holistic approach to SEO, encompassing these diverse strategies, will often yield far more impressive results than merely banking on the age of your domain alone. A practical tip is to regularly review analytics to see which strategies are working, and don't hesitate to adapt as you learn what resonates best with your audience.

15. Building a Sustainable SEO Plan

15.1 The Importance of Consistency in SEO

Just like cultivating a garden, SEO is not a one-time project but rather an ongoing commitment. When I first started focusing on SEO for my website, I quickly realized that sporadic efforts wouldn't yield the desired results. I learned that to genuinely benefit from search engine optimization, I needed to maintain a steady pace. Implementing small, regular updates to my content and continually optimizing my website's performance made a noticeable difference over time. By making these practices a part of my routine, I saw improved rankings and increased organic traffic. This tuning of the SEO engine took patience, but the cumulative effect of consistency built a strong foundation on which my online presence could thrive.

One effective way to build this consistency is by creating a content calendar. This doesn't have to be complex; even a simple spreadsheet mapping out weekly or monthly topics can help you stay accountable. For instance, I set a goal to write and publish a new blog post every two weeks. Not only did this regularity help in creating fresh content, but it also signaled to search engines that my site was active. Ensuring your site is properly optimized—through regular updates to keywords, meta tags, and alt texts—is another method to maintain consistency. Furthermore, monitoring your analytics consistently allows you to track what works and adjust strategies as necessary, rather than waiting months to realize something is amiss. Consistency in SEO isn't just about routine; it's about adaptation and continual refinement.

Finally, one of the most important things I've learned is that consistency breeds trust, both with your audience and search engines. When visitors know they can rely on you for fresh, valuable content, they're more likely to return and share your site with others, which enhances your credibility. This trust translates to higher rankings, as search engines favor sites that provide consistent, high-quality experiences for users. A practical tip is to set specific, measurable goals for your SEO efforts. For instance, aim to increase your site's domain authority incrementally over a few months. By setting these benchmarks, I found myself more engaged in the process and able to clearly evaluate the impact of my consistent efforts. Quality content, reliable updates, and engagement with your audience are the cornerstones of a successful SEO strategy that stands the test of time.

15.2 Balancing Short-Term and Long-Term Strategies

 It's easy to get caught up in the immediate needs of running a website or a small business, where last-minute tasks and urgent calls for attention demand our focus. Yet, while those short-term victories can provide a rush of satisfaction, they can sometimes lead us to overlook the broader picture of where we want to go in the future. I've learned that it's essential to keep an eye on both ends of the spectrum. Short-term strategies often require quick actions and rapid results, but these should ideally feed into our long-term aspirations. For instance, boosting website traffic through a temporary promotion can be beneficial, but it's vital to ensure that those visitors are also being nurtured into loyal customers who will return by aligning this tactic with a broader content marketing strategy. The key is to be intentional; each short-term win should connect strategically to the larger objectives of your business.

Designing a strategy that incorporates both short-term and long-term elements effectively requires a structured approach. Start by identifying your long-term vision—what you ultimately want your website or business to achieve. Then, think about the milestones that will lead you there. From my experience, breaking down that vision into smaller, actionable steps can be incredibly effective. This means creating a timeline where short-term actions dominate at the initial stages but gradually align with the overarching aims. For example, if your long-term goal is to establish authority in your niche, your short-term strategies might include guest blogging or engaging more on social media to build awareness. As you progress, these actions will not only produce immediate engagement but also contribute to your long-term credibility. Always assess the metrics from your short-term strategies, using those insights to refine and adjust your long-term plan.

As you navigate the tension between immediate results and future aspirations, consider one practical tip: implement a feedback loop. Regularly evaluate the results of your short-term strategies and how they affect your long-term goals. This reflection allows you to pivot when something isn't resonating, ensuring you remain agile and responsive to the market's needs while still moving toward your vision. Balancing these two aspects doesn't have to be daunting. It's about setting the right framework that allows your daily actions to illuminate the path forward, always keeping your eyes on the ultimate destination. Practice patience, but don't forget to celebrate those small victories along the way, as they can be vital stepping stones toward your larger ambitions.

15.3 Keeping abreast of Industry Trends and Changes

In today's fast-paced digital environment, where search engines like Google frequently change algorithms and introduce new features, having your finger on the pulse can make all the difference. For instance, understanding how user experience plays into search rankings or how mobile optimization is more crucial than ever can directly impact your website's visibility. With discussions around topics like voice search, local SEO, and artificial intelligence in search, it's essential to grasp these trends so you can adapt your strategies accordingly. Ignoring these shifts puts you at risk of falling behind your competitors who are more agile in their tactics and strategies related to SEO.

Discovering resources and practices for keeping in touch with evolving SEO landscapes is a continual journey. One of the most effective ways I find to stay informed is by subscribing to industry-leading blogs and newsletters. Resources like Moz, Search Engine Journal, and Neil Patel's blog provide valuable insights and updates. Moreover, attending webinars or online courses related to SEO can also enhance your knowledge and skills. Engaging with communities on platforms like Reddit or LinkedIn can foster discussions that expose you to different viewpoints and practical experiences. Networking with other small business owners or webmasters can uncover local trends that are specific to your industry, giving you an edge in crafting your SEO approach. Remember that the digital landscape is constantly shifting, so dedicating time each week to learning and adapting can help ensure that your website remains competitive and relevant.

It's helpful to remember that being proactive about these changes can save you time and resources in the long run. Implementing an SEO audit regularly allows you to measure the effectiveness of your strategies in relation to these industry trends. This way, instead of reacting after changes are made, you can anticipate and incorporate elements of emerging trends into your existing strategy. Being aware of industry conferences and following thought leaders on social media are also excellent methods to learn about future changes that can affect you. Engaging with this information not only positions you to optimize effectively but also cultivates a mindset of continual improvement, ensuring that your website never becomes stagnant but continues to evolve with the industry.

16. Importance of SEO Consulting

16.1 The Importance of Good SEO Consulting

When I first dived into the world of online business, I quickly realized that having a great website wasn't enough; I needed to ensure it was visible to my target audience. This is where SEO consultants come into play. They bring expertise that goes beyond basic search engine optimization tactics. A good consultant can analyze your current website performance, identify areas of improvement, and suggest strategies that align with your specific business goals. They don't just throw generic advice at you; they take the time to understand the nuances of your industry and how it operates in the digital landscape. Each suggestion is backed by data, which means that you're not just guessing what might work, but you're following a well-researched plan designed to elevate your online presence.

Understanding when and how to leverage consulting services can greatly benefit your SEO strategy. It's not just about hiring a consultant at the beginning of your journey; the timing and context of when you seek help matter significantly. For instance, if you've noticed that your website traffic has plateaued or even declined, a consultant can provide fresh perspectives that might reveal unseen obstacles or missed opportunities. They can also assist with advanced strategies like content marketing or technical SEO when your business starts scaling, ensuring that your site continues to grow alongside your audience. The relationship with a good consultant should be collaborative—it's beneficial to keep communicative lines open, so they understand not only your current goals but also your long-term vision. An effective SEO consulting engagement will empower you with the knowledge and tools necessary to maintain and enhance your SEO tactics long after the consultation is over. To maximize your investment, consider integrating regular check-ins with your consultant to stay updated on evolving trends and best practices in SEO.

16.2 About Author

With over a decade of hands-on experience in the world of search engine optimization, I have dedicated my career to mastering the intricate dynamics of digital marketing. My journey began when I launched my first website, motivated by a passion for technology and a desire to connect with others. From the early days of clunky HTML and rudimentary SEO techniques, I immersed myself in understanding how search engines work, tirelessly studying algorithms and ranking factors. I learned through trial and error, optimizing my site and watching how each change impacted its visibility. This experience catalyzed my deep-seated expertise in SEO. I have worked with a diverse array of clients—from small local businesses trying to establish their online presence to larger corporations seeking to enhance their competitive edge. Throughout this journey, I have absorbed a wealth of knowledge about the best practices and strategies that consistently yield results.

The driving force behind my commitment to sharing effective SEO strategies stems from a broader vision: I genuinely believe that every website has the potential to thrive in the online ecosystem. I have seen firsthand how a well-optimized site can transform a business, elevating it from obscurity to a recognizable brand in its niche. My motivation comes from helping others achieve similar success and demystifying the complexities of SEO. I want to empower website owners, small business entrepreneurs, and webmasters, equipping them with practical techniques and insights that will help them navigate the often confusing world of search engine rankings. It's vital for me to break down these concepts into layman's terms, making them accessible and actionable for anyone who seeks to enhance their online visibility. This book is a culmination of my experiences and insights, crafted to guide you through the evolving landscape of SEO with clarity and confidence.

As you delve into the strategies laid out in the following sections, remember to keep your audience at the forefront of your mind. SEO is not just about keywords and analytics; it's about creating a valuable experience for your users. Always ask yourself: how can the information I provide resonate with my audience? When you align your strategies with their needs and interests, you increase your chances of success. Embrace the journey of learning and growing in SEO, and you will inevitably find your own path to online success.